The Giant's Garden

Written by Jenny Feely

Illustrated by Naomi Lewis

Flying Start
to Literacy®

Contents

Chapter 1
A giant comes to town

When the Giant came to live at Hayfield farm the people in the nearby village came to greet him.

"Welcome to our village, Giant," they said. "We hope we can all be friends."

"Hmmph!" said the Giant. "I don't see how that can happen. People don't like giants and giants don't like people."

The Giant turned his back, stomped into the farmhouse and slammed the door.

"What an unfriendly giant," said the villagers. "It is no surprise that people don't like giants. We certainly won't come out here again!"

And one by one the villagers turned away. All except Harriet.

"That giant needs a friend," she said.

But no one was listening.

Harriet looked over the fence at the Giant's garden. There were lots of weeds and they were growing everywhere. This gave Harriet an idea.

Harriet hurried back to town to get some things.

Chapter 2
Planting a new idea

In no time at all Harriet was back at the Giant's farm. She reached up and knocked on his door.

She waited and waited.

Just as Harriet was about to turn and go, the door opened. The Giant stood, looking down at her.

"Go away," he said.

"I will go away," said Harriet. "But before I go, could I just put these plants into your garden?"

Harriet had lots of plants with her.

"I have been growing lots of seeds at home and I have too many plants for my little garden," said Harriet. "I need to plant them somewhere before they die. Could I plant them in your garden?"

"Hmmph!" said the Giant. "If you have to."

And he shut the door.

Harriet dug and dug until all the
weeds were gone.

Then she planted her plants.

The Giant watched Harriet from
his window.

Chapter 3
A helping hand

The next day Harriet came to water her plants.

"Hello," she said to the Giant who was sitting on the wall near the garden.

"Mmm," said the Giant.

Harriet filled the watering can. She tried to pick it up, but it was too heavy.

Then a big hand closed over hers.

"Let me do that," said the Giant,
as he easily lifted the watering can.

From then on, Harriet and the
Giant worked together in the garden
every day. And every day the Giant
smiled a little more and had a little
more to say.

Chapter 4
Something blossoms

Soon there were flowers everywhere. Harriet had planted flowers that brought hundreds of butterflies to the garden.

A butterfly landed on the Giant's nose and the Giant laughed out loud.

"This garden is lovely," said the Giant. "Do you think we could make another garden in the field?"

"Of course," said Harriet. "You can make a garden anywhere."

"Will you help me?" said the Giant.

"Of course I will," said Harriet. "That's what friends are for."

In the field next to the farmhouse
Harriet and the Giant made an
animal garden.

The Giant made wire frames shaped
like animals for plants to grow on.

Harriet snipped the plants as they grew.

Soon the field had lots of green
animals all over it.

Then Harriet and the Giant planted some corn. They put the seeds in rows that went down the field and across the field.

As the corn grew tall and strong, it became a maze. Harriet and the Giant played hide and seek in the maze.

They made a floating garden on the pond. It was filled with flowers that floated on the top of the water.

And they even planted a garden on the walls of the Giant's farmhouse.

"The garden on the walls will make your house cool in summer and warm in winter," said Harriet.

"This garden is grand," said the Giant.

"It is," said Harriet. "Let's have a garden party and invite all the villagers."

The Giant looked sad. "They won't come," he said. "People don't like giants."

"They would if they knew you the way I do," said Harriet.

Chapter 5
A mystery trail

Harriet picked a bunch of flowers from the Giant's garden. She left a flower and a note on the doorsteps of everyone in the village.

Be in the village square this Friday at 3pm. Follow the flower trail and make a new friend.

On Friday at 3 o'clock all the villagers were waiting.

"Where are we going?" the villagers asked.

"You will see," said Harriet, and off she walked, following the flower trail.

When the villagers got to the Giant's farm they couldn't believe their eyes.

"Welcome," said the Giant. "Come and enjoy the beautiful garden that my good friend Harriet and I have made together."

"Amazing!" whispered the people to each other. "A giant has made friends with a person and a person has made friends with a giant!"

The villagers marvelled at the animal garden and played hide and seek in the maze.

They rowed boats around the floating garden and giggled when butterflies landed on them in the butterfly garden.

All too soon it was time to go home.

"Thank you for coming," said the Giant.
"Come again soon."

"We certainly will," said the villagers.
"It is good to spend time with friends."

And all the villagers went off to make
their own gardens.